Ramblings of a Fool

Yamil Ortega Rios

BookLeaf Publishing

India | USA | UK

Presentation by *BookLeaf Publishing*

Web: www.bookleafpub.com

E-mail: info@bookleafpub.com

ISBN: 9789357213929

First edition 2022

ACKNOWLEDGEMENT

To the people that I may or may not have loved.
I still don't know who you are.

PREFACE

Love is a complex emotion; sometimes, it feels as though you have experienced love many times. And other times, it may feel like love is like a stranger whom you have never been acquainted with. In this collection of poetry, I detail some of the confounding experiences that I have had with love. Perhaps, you have felt this way as well.

Not Galatae

You are you
Not some man made maiden
Or some vision of what seems to be ideal
Eyes that rest on you see something that is real
Not formed by the clay of public opinion
You have been you from the beginning
You have a traits that many desire
You are somebody that I greatly admire
You carry the confidence of Aphrodite
Your spirit shows the strength of Artemis
Your heart was not touched by King Midas
For it is worth far more than gold

And as I write these words while I think of you
I realize now that I am Pygmalion
You are a vision that will never reach my hopes
Carefully crafted conjectures that cannot be
conceived
You are no Galatae
My words and my hopes cannot be brought to
life
You are an simply an idea that cause my heart
strife
You will forever stay as a dream inside my brain
An Athena that will not spring from my head

Forever trapped inside my heart and soul
Words on a page-- making me unwhole
A sculpture forever on a pedestal
You are not you

Happy Birthday!

Wake up staring at the ceiling
Time flies- bye-
Still have a miasmic feeling
Blink, Blink- sigh-
Another day

Struggle- to get out of bed
Consumed by dread
Never felt before
At this point, I'd even take the floor
Is this the feeling of 24

Blink, blink- sigh-
The alarm emanates
Five minutes- snooze-
Ten minutes- snooze-
Is this...
Deep Rest?

Another Stupid Love Poem

I have never had the feeling
Where my heart begins to sing
I have asked those who have
Felt that embrace from Cupid
Questions to try and understand.
What does it feel to be in love?
Help my poor brain comprehend
Please! Please, my dear friend
Show me a hand that you can lend!
I beg you; I beg you, Eros!
Pierce me with your arrows!
Unless? Of course, of course!
How could I not think of this before?
Much like Aphrodite,
And other gods and goddesses,
Love is a myth!
Am I a fool for not having seen it before?
This is not a love poem
Is there even such a thing?

Run or Die

Run-
And don't stop running until you
Die-
For you, that is the only way you'll ever
Fly-
And if you cannot force your legs to move,
Crawl-
Do what you can to prevent the
Fall-
For in this world you have to
Fight-
To wander in a weary world of
Fright-
Do this, and so much, more to stay
Alive-
You have to do this to
Survive

To Icarus, Who Flew Too Close to the Sun

Wax wings that wasted away
left you to fall to the earth
after flying to the light of day
because you knew your worth
Like a flame that burns quick,
your pride put you at risk

I cannot fall to my demise
For I am too cowardly to ever rise
Too fearful to try to fly
and touch the bright blue sky
Scared to fail and hit the ground
Or worse, to die like you, and drown

Fear is the enemy of mine
Who put me in jail to confine
and left me there to resign
myself to a life on the decline

Ahh, to be like Icarus and to fly
To not waste my life and die
Icarus, you flew too close to the sun
a mistake that will not be redone

Memories That You Left

Do you think of me
like I think of you?
Do you reminisce
of the things that I miss?
The laughs that we shared-
or are your memories pared?

Will you remember me when I am gone?
Or will your life simply carry on?
For your own sake, my dear-
I hope your memory of me is unclear
For those beautiful perceptions
have left me with nothing but obsessions

Tears are all that are left
now that you've stolen
my heart from my chest

The Arrow I Shot

My life is like an arrow
It was nocked and shot-
Sent in a single direction
With a true intention
that I knew not
for my mind was too narrow

Where did you go
after you left my bow?
You keep moving forward;
Is it where I had ordered?
Or did you stray, my friend,
before you reached the end?

Sweet Dreams

Sweet dream are oft worse than nightmares-
Although they are full of scares,
you have the luxury to escape from there-
When pretty dreams end, they make you shake-
For they are so beautiful, you wish to never
wake
and resume your life in a world full of mistakes
Our mind gives us a merciful world to cope
to forget this world which has no hope-
So I curse damn dreams
and hope for nightmares

Three of a Kind

The first one showed me friendship
That disappears with age
Lashed my soul with a leather whip
Left in a deep, dark ditch

The second taught me about love
Unrequited, though it was
She gave my heart a merry shove
Plummeted to the pit

The last one bewilders the brain
Not knowing how to feel
She has not gifted me with pain
But time ticks down, down, down

Eden on Earth

I did not visit the Garden of Eden
Nor did I see the sights in Elysium
But, to me, none of that mattered
For me, Heaven and Earth were connected
Until one day, near the rivers that flowed,
I saw a daisy dancing in the road
That beautiful little wonder
That made me stop and ponder
And as I walked closer and closer
And knelt to get a better view
I saw the rivers that had once been clear
Turn into a stream of scarlet red
My eyes widened with terror and fear
And filled my soul with dread
I plucked the daisy from the ground
Full of paranoia, I looked around
The sky was crying bloody tears
I heard a noise that split my ears
Stomping boots that raged against world
I saw the smoke that twisted and twirled
And as I gazed upon the flower
And I saw the ruined petals
I closed my eyes to make me blind
And suddenly, a thought escaped my mind
"Paradise is forever Lost"

Forever

Until forever falls apart
You shall be in my heart
And though that time seems far away
You shall be there for the ends of days
And though forever may not last
When I'm near you my heart beats fast
And through the fields we shall sing
A song of love—so mesmerizing

The View from Up There

It must be nice
To look from above
To see the world
From among the clouds
To forget the pains
On the ground where it rains

How is it up there?
From below it seems nice
Down here, nothing is fair
And suffering is dealt twice
Enjoy The View from Up There
Enjoy your paradise
I hope the admission was worth the price

The Rose that Heaven Forgot

Why are you sitting alone
It is peculiar to me
Seeing you by stone and tree
When you could be with the rest
Up here, with the blessed
Do you think they forgot
And left you to rot
Well, I certainly did not
Pretty rose in that spot
I will leave this domain
And travel to your plain
I swear to you, love
By the gods up above
I will never leave you again

No Llores Por Mi

No gastes tus lágrimas
Llorando por mi

Those tears would be a loss
And could fill an empty sea

El tiempo que toma limpiarlos
No vale el esfuerzo

You stain a face that's grandiose
So don't let those tears flow

Olvidame y yo tratare
De olvidarme de ti

So don't let your tears fall away
Or you shall never be free

Honesty

When is a person the most honest they can be?
They are the most truthful when they are
desperate
As the eye can see.
You see their truth when they slur their speech
They feel that they are a leech
They tell the truth when they feel their worst
And poison spews from their words
The world spins for them
When they close their eyes
And then they cry
They tell the stories they would never dare tell
If they were to be feeling well
And so, you hear their tales
And comfort them the best you can
But you hate them
For their poison has begun to seep into your
system
And their honesty has somehow made you their
victim

Dead Thoughts

Thoughts left unsaid
Are better of dead
Words loaded with regret
Do nothing but beset
You with feelings that harm
And leave you with discharm
So keep remorse to yourself
And I'll keep mine to myself

Those Who Walk Among Us

They say that Hell is other people
And this fact, it may be true
But there is hope for me
Because I walk along with you
There are those who walk among us
Who make life a living blaze
But I am with you, and thus,
All my problems are a haze
There are those who walk among us
But you are not in that flock
Who makes me wish that time
Would expire from the clock
I am ashamed to say that I'm unable
To make life for you more stable
They say that Hell is other people
And this fact, it may be true;
But I believe that I am Hell too

In Love With the Voice of the Dead

I have fallen for words that were written long
ago
Transcribed by candlelight are lyrics that echo
The verses still seem to dance upon the page
And my appreciation continues to grow with age

You promised wild nights for you and me
You promised love would give life immortality
I look upon the words you wrote
Poems that I learn by rote
Bashing against my skull I hear
A voice that comes through clear

I write my script to commune with you
To immortalize my hearts desires
Perhaps one day we will meet to
Sing with the angel choirs

Ode To Ignorance

To those that loved
and lost
and never loved again
My heart goes out
to you
For you have lived
and died
and will never live again
It is better to live
in ignorance
than to have felt the warm embrace
of love
Now, you struggle without its bliss
Not knowing
is infinitely better that to
have loved
and lost
and never
loved again

We are All the Same

Did he know where he was
When he first fell in love
Or was his life just a blur
When he first laid eyes on her

Did you know what you were feeling
Did you ever know anything
Or were your emotions wild and haphazard
When you first became enamored

Did I know or recognize this warmth
Which transfigured my heart into a storm
When I looked into your grey eyes
This moment that feels so long ago
Which makes me realize how fast time flies
He, you, and I were all dealt the same blow

The End

Books start
Films start
Songs start
Poems start

I don't know how this will end
Many things come to their close
And, it is said, that if a door closes
Another one will open
But when will the door stay shut?
It is always easy to start
But when it comes to an end,
It is difficult to create art
And when creating something-
Something to be proud of-
Is the perfect end locked within the heart?
The start chooses us-
We have no choice-
When it comes to the end
Do we have a voice
As for life-
Well-

Books end
Films end

Songs end
Poems end

Life… ends